MW00977351

HOW TO WIN GIRLS &

INFLUENCE WOMEN

(Easy Guide for Beginners)

By

Romeo Montaje

Copyright 2010 – Romeo Montaje

All rights reserved. No part of this book may be reproduced in any form or by any electronic or mechanical means including information storage and retrieval systems, without permission in writing from the author. The only exception is by a reviewer, who may quote short excerpts in a review.

Disclaimer:

This book provides suggestions only and how the reader uses it is their choice. The authors / publishers are not liable for inappropriate use of the information by the reader.

CONTENTS

2.12 How to have good manners?

<u>Section 3: Meeting women - Page 42</u>

3.1 How to meet women?

3.2 How to pick-up women randomly?

3.3 How to approach a woman in public settings?

3.4 How to look approachable in front of women?

3.5 How to have a happy face?

3.6 How to draw attention of women?

3.7 How to act around women?

3.8 How to get to know someone while remaining Mysterious yourself?

<u>Section 4: Understanding women – Page 62</u>

4.1. What creates attraction in women?

4.2. How to read a woman's body language?

4.3 How to know if a woman likes you?

4.4 How to attract a woman older than you?

Section 5: Talking to women – Page 83

Section 6: Dating – Page 100

6.14 How to date on a budget?

<u>Section 7: Getting Physical – Page 122</u>

7.1 How to break the touch barrier?

7.2 How to make the first move?

7.3 How to have a first Kiss?

7.4 How to Romantically hug a woman?

<u>Section 8: Rejection & Confidence - Page 128</u>

8.1 How to handle rejection?

8.2 How to overcome the fear of rejection?

8.3 How to get over rejection?

8.4 How to tell when you may have been rejected by a woman?

8.5 How to move on after rejection?

8.6 How to regain confidence after rejection ?

<u>Section 9: Conclusion – Page 140</u>

Section 1: Introduction

The primary reason for writing this beginner's guidebook is that a lot of readers feel the existing HOW TO books on Seduction are often quite complicated. They focus too much on borrowed pickup routines. Many people feel these routines do not fit into their personality. On the other hand there are some books which are too short and incomplete and do not cover the whole spectrum of seduction. There is hardly anything in between these two extremes. That is where this book fits in.

This is a easy practical guide which tries to give real-life instead of theoretical examples. I wrote it to focus on the practical circumstances of life and taking into consideration the initial anxiety involved in picking up women. You can always read more complicated stuff after finishing this book. This book will teach you how to survive in the real world of seducing women.

"Always be a first-rate version of yourself,
instead of a second-rate version of somebody else."
- Judy Garland

Work on developing your own 'Self" and create your own
pick-up 'Game'.

This is the only method of this book. The goal is to help
the normal, healthy and well-adjusted males form lasting
relationship with similar females as the human beings as
they are. This book is concise and covers all essential
tools to create your own strategies to win & influence
females. In today's mass market there are lots of books
on Pickup techniques mainly for short term gains. Most
of them try to teach some secret robotic formula whereby
they suggest that you change your personality drastically
and fit into some typical Pickup Artist's (PUA) routine.
Another problem is that most of these PUA routines are
based on rather simplistic assumption that women have
poor intelligence and they can be manipulated easily by

personality disordered males looking for short term sexual gains. I am not criticizing these methods. However it up to the judgment of the reader to decide what is best for them.

Personally I am of the opinion that it is not easy to be someone different within a few months after reading a book! Sometimes trying to copy another person is the hardest thing to do and it can make us more disadvantaged in the dating scene. Social and psychological research has shown that trying to emulate someone else's personality is very stressful and it can seriously handicap our own self-esteem in the dating scene.

No man deserves to be single if it makes him unhappy. Having said that, through this book I am doing my bit to help people change their 'luck'. This book is meant to help those males who find it hard to win females or influence them. I work in mental health and have particular interest in human relationships. As part of my job I have been involved in counseling people who have social anxiety when it comes to dating.

My strong view is that it is not easy to change ourselves drastically overnight just by reading a book. Therefore my approach is to help you identify your inner strengths and build up on your strengths to make you a confident and attractive person in the eyes of the opposite sex. So regarding this book I can only say that it is not going to teach you any secret formula. Rather it is a guide book on how to develop your sense of 'Self' and use it to your advantage to win girls and influence women for long term gains. It will teach you vital social skills and psychological techniques which work with most psychologically healthy women. Use it to win over only women that you have a genuine interest in.

By reading this book you are likely to 'learn' how to feel more confident when you are trying to interact with women. This is a very concise pocket book which is easy to read and understand. The message is written in simple straight-forward language. I am sure those who read this book will find the knowledge helpful and will be way ahead of other straight men in the competitive world of dating women.

All men need women because they are just there for us! So do not be ashamed of your desire to win them, remember that is what they also want and need. Just think of it like this - by showing interest in them you are actually doing them a favor. Go out and enjoy the journey.

Finally two fundamental tips - never ever focus too seriously on any single woman at one point of time when you are practicing your skills, and also be prepared to ignore rejection. Its all about the number game!

The ultimate reason for any man's success with women is

his ability to learn from experience and progressively sharpen his social skills to perfection. In dating, like in anything else, you have to play the game if you want to become a master. Forget any fears you might have and get down to action. Persistent practice will maximize your chances of success. Remember the age old saying: Fortune favors the brave. As Casanova put it so well in his work "Timidity is often another word for stupidity."

Build upon your strengths and slowly you will see your courage and confidence increasing. As Norman Pearle wrote: "People become really quite remarkable when they start thinking that they can do things. When they believe in themselves they have the first secret to success." ....So good luck my friend!

Section 2: Preparing Self

2.1 Why are you reading this Book?

I want you to ask yourself this question. Obviously you want to help your self. But are you really serious about it? Are you willing to put in the **time and effort** to develop yourself into a 'Casanova' for women? If so then keep reading....

First let us examine 'what is' the **biggest challenge** facing us when we try to pick-up women. It is our **fear of rejection**. In life we are all brought up under different circumstances. These do affect our sense of self-confidence. People who have been unlucky in social relationships or had some traumatic experiences may have lost their self-confidence along the way. This is a natural thing to happen and so do not blame yourself. It is never too late.

In this book we will work together hand in hand to **develop your strengths** and **restore your sense of healthy self image**. This is important because unless we all feel confident under our own skin, we will always be disadvantaged in the dating game.

In this book we take a **humanistic approach** to restore our self–confidence first and then learn the psychological techniques of social interaction with women.

I have tried to keep this book **concise and simple** because we know that in our busy life we do not have a lot of time to read and process a large amount of complicated information. This book is keeping with this requirement of the twenty-first century man. It is a summary of techniques based on positive social interactions between men and women. The facts have been organized in a realistic way with **bold highlighting** to make it easy to read. There are no gimmicks or secret methods. It is all about developing and applying your own self as you are - but the best of your own self.

Picking-up women is like a **number game**. In the world of dating 'you' are the commodity and your job is to sell yourself to the best of your ability. For this you need a practical and effective marketing plan. There will be rejections, but it is important to keep persisting. Eventually **practice** will make you **perfect** in your marketing strategy. In time a point will come when you will know exactly what to say or do in order to get the best results for yourself.

Always remember the age old wise saying – "**there are plenty of fish is the sea**". Here 'fish' stands for possibilities (or potential mates). This is an eternal truth. Take this to heart and the rest will all fall in its own place.

2.2 Why do you want a woman?

Because **nature** has programmed man in this way. It is

one of our **basic needs**. Trying to suppress that need will only create stress within us. That will make us unhappy. So it is okay to accept that you are looking and may be not finding the right woman. However you must keep yourself motivated to continue your search. **Nothing will happen just by chance.** Only action on your part can set the ball rolling. Just to keep your motivation level up, think of all the reasons you would want to have a woman by your side. Then write them down and keep it in front of you. Every time you feel like motivating yourself, go through the list. Keep it up-to date so that there is relevance to your current life situation. Some of the key advantages include sharing your life, getting emotional fulfillment and of-course sexual pleasure. At the end of the day it is all about creating the right mind set within you – and the rest will all follow. So **keep your self - motivation level high.** Many men remain single because they give up easily – please do not fall into that trap.

2.3 What is unpleasant about your life that you can

change?

Generally speaking, many people who are single often feel **lonely**. Being lonely can in turn reduce our sense of self-confidence. We can then start feeling more insecure around women. This is like a vicious cycle. Loneliness leads to poor self-confidence, which leads to poor self-esteem, which leads to feelings of insecurity, which leads to more loneliness, which leads to more unhappiness – and the cycle goes on and on. Many people try to justify themselves by saying - 'being single does not mean I am lonely'. Well yes and no. At times we all feel the need to have a member of the opposite sex in our life. We may be ignoring this but deep down if we look into our inner self, we will realize this truth. We are all human beings and we are born with certain **basic instincts**. It creates a lot of **stress** when we try to suppress our natural instincts. Rather it is easier to accept the reality and work towards meeting our emotional and physical needs. It is okay to accept that being single can be lonely at times. Unless we

accept our inner desires, we will not be able to make changes to our lives. Therefore it is important for us to prepare ourselves psychologically for this task in hand. Although there is no quick fix solution to this problem, however it is still a very achievable goal if we apply certain common sense principles. We may not want to spend our life being single while most of the others are enjoying life with their partners. No certainly not. I am not at all suggesting that it is okay to be single especially if you have a need within you. **Do not try to repress your desire** as it will make you more stressed. Rather accept the reality and **work towards fulfilling that desire.**

2.4 What is stopping you from finding women?

Fear of rejection. This is the biggest mental block that we need to overcome. Rejection hurts us because it **creates** a lot of **shame** within us. Of-course anyone would be afraid to some extent because no one wants to be rejected. Rejection hurts our sense of self-worth. It can demoralize us and if we take it very seriously, it can prevent us from picking-up women in future. So we should rather accept the feeling of **fear as normal** and then work on strategies to **overcome this**. As we all know – picking-up women is a number game. If we keep trying, we will surely become experts in marketing ourselves successfully. As you start taking small steps towards overcoming your fear, slowly and gradually you will be able to **desensitize** yourself against it. This will increase your self-confidence – but do it at your **own pace**! Too much of rejection over a short time can be more harmful for your self-worth. Depending on your level of expertise, work according to your own pace. This is the **best approach** that I recommend.

Once you begin to think of dating as a '**Numbers Game**', you can start to have as many dates as you want - depending on how many women you approach. It is true that people who are least bothered by rejection are able to persist with their game more vigorously. As they keep trying, they become expert 'sales-persons' and this is essentially the secret of their success. People who are physically attractive can have a slight advantage initially but others can beat them by developing charismatic personality. All scientific research shows that **personality is the most important factor in attracting women!** In this book our emphasis would be to learn how to build a '**naturally**' charming and charismatic personality.

Although I do accept that even when you're thinking about the numbers, it still hurts to be rejected. However, I can tell you that most women would be **extremely gracious** in rejecting men who treat them with care and respect. Usually they are flattered that you have bothered to ask them out, even if they aren't interested!

2.5 How to develop courage to approach women?

It is not easy to move out of our **comfort zone**. Our

comfort zone is like a wall around us. It prevents our 'sense of Self' from being hurt or upset. We tend to use it to defend our sense of Self. However when we are trying to pick-up girls, it is imperative for us to **come out** of this comfort zone. I agree that it is challenging but what else to do? If we do not step out of this little area of comfort – we will **miss out** on many pleasurable opportunities. Therefore we need to **prepare** ourselves **mentally** to face the **challenge**. We will learn to do that by exploring ways of acquiring courage to begin with. Remember 'Healthy challenges help us to build courage and confidence.' Here are the tips on how to feel courageous & confident in front of women. Learn to **accept yourself** whole-heartedly and be yourself. Accept your **uniqueness** and **forgive** yourself for any shortcomings you may think you have. This will go a long way to help you become yourself. **No one can be perfect** – we are all a mixture of good and bad. There are ways of polishing our physical appearance – but essentially it all boils down to whether we feel good about ourselves or not. Only when we start to accept our sense of Self as it is – neither bad not good, then only can we go **beyond any inferiority or superiority complex**. You will find that once you start accepting yourself wholeheartedly, you will be projecting **courage and confidence** everywhere you go. Be **pleasant and respectful** to everyone. Your positive attitude towards others will give you a lot of moral courage. This will translate into self-confidence. Remember any challenge is frightening and to step out of your comfort zone is a natural cause of anxiety. However if you view every challenge as a **opportunity for growth** – an opportunity to improve your social skills, you will feel much more relaxed. As you push yourself you will find surprisingly that you can do it. It does not matter what the outcome is, remember it always pays to be good-natured. Some people may advice you that it is better to project arrogance in order to pick-up girls. But all research shows that there is difference between being arrogant and being self-respecting. You need to be pleasant and yet not project yourself as a pushover. Your attitude should show that you are **appreciating** the presence of the woman in front of you **without being needy or desperate**. When you are in social situations with women around do not show hesitation when you talk to them. Be spontaneous and good-natured towards her and everyone else. A gracious person is always confident because his sense of goodness gives him inner courage to be forgiving and accepting of others as they are. If you see someone whom you like, go and get her attention. **No point in hesitating – be spontaneous.** Go for it. If you hesitate to think, your fear will take control of your emotions. It will paralyze you. Rather be yourself and present a nice friendly picture of yourself. A very casual and natural approach!

2.6 How to appear confident?

The most important attribute of any man in any social situation is his confidence because that is the first thing others see. But when we have to step outside our comfort zone it is not easy. Naturally we will feel nervous. However we can still **create the impression** of being confident by using our **body language**. That is what the **actors** have been doing for ages in the movies. It is not hard once you know how to present yourself and follow the instructions given. Hold head up high and have an upright **posture**. Make good **eye contact**. Don't look down or from side to side. **Smile** politely. Always show your pleasant personality. **Speak clearly** and slowly. Do not speak rapidly – it is a sign of nervousness. If you have to shake hands, have a firm and yet gentle grip. Ask general questions, do not get too personal with any stranger. **Laugh and use humor** – even at your own mistakes. It shows a sign of confidence. Don't just stand in one place, **move around** and say hello to people. Be **open and honest** in your attitude. **Appreciate yourself for who you are**.

2.7 How to overcome nervousness while you are in front of the woman?

Now let us look at a common scenario. You have approached a woman and started conversation. What if suddenly you feel a **rush of anxiety**. You feel over-conscious about yourself. Well, this is a normal thing which can happen to all of us in the initial stages of challenging social interactions. To overcome this feeling is quite possible if we follow the steps described below. First is to **be yourself** and **not try to impress** her at this point. Remember the harder one tries to impress people, the more unimpressed they become. Even if you do not feel confident at this point, **no one else knows it**. So fake it until you make it. Pretend to be confident and eventually you will become confident. Try and look as genuine as possible, then you will also start to feel the same. These actions will tell your subconscious mind that you are special and valuable, and this in turn, will truly make you confident in yourself. Act as though you are not worried about what other people think (even if you do). In any conversation be honest and open. Remember that your **honest attitude**, your **natural beliefs** and the **outpouring of life energy** within you always reaches and enter the hearts of other people. It is because of your own attachment to pettiness and superficial glamor and glitter that you underestimate yourself. So be sure that if you do soul searching and act accordingly, people will surely think that you are confident. Sometimes when you act confident **other people can get envious**. In a social situation someone may try to pull you down. Just learn to ignore such comments without being angry. Take this as a tip that what you are doing is working. It will show the women that you are cool!

2.8 How to avoid looking over confident?

Being confident is attractive, but being **over confident** is not. It is important to understand the difference. As human beings we are never perfect. But sometimes we try too hard to project ourselves as perfect. This can be a **turn off.** Instead of appearing confident one may actually appear ridiculous. Here are a few tips to remember. **Do not be too loud, arrogant or demanding**. That is a turn off for most women. **Don't appear clingy.** This will make them feel like you're not needed. **Do not try too hard** to make others think that you are confident. That will make people think, feel, and confirm that you are ridiculous rather than confident. Don't over do the smiling bit. Some people say you have to smile all the time but that can come off as kind of offensive. **Just do what comes naturally** and smile at appropriate times. Don't be discouraged if you can't follow certain steps like maintaining a perfect posture. You don't have to have 'perfect' posture to be respected. **Just be comfortable under your own skin.**

2.9 How to be yourself in front of women?

Being yourself at all times is important because it shows that you are not hiding who you are or changing things about you to fit in. However it does not mean you are trying to big note yourself. There is a big difference. Being yourself is all about **celebrating yourself (the inner self)** by feeling happy with who you are. Celebrating the uniqueness in you – the fact that there is no-one else in this universe who is exactly same as you. Isn't that a fascinating way of looking at your own existence! Like Oscar Wilde, the famous writer, said "*Be yourself; everyone else is already taken.*" Read these tips on how to be comfortable with your own self at all times (including those when you are with women). Learn how to express the inner you.

Finding meaning in your existence: It means understanding and accepting yourself. Look at it like this – how can others accept you if you are not able to accept yourself? In your spare time think over who you are – what you think of yourself. Think of how you can improve your inner self. Accept all the mistakes that you may have done and forgive yourself. This will give you a new meaning of life.

Stop worrying about how she perceives you: The fact is, it really doesn't matter. It's impossible to be yourself when you're caught up in wondering what she is thinking of you. To be yourself, you've got to let go of these concerns and just let yourself flow, with only your consideration of others as a filter — not *their* consideration of you. Besides, if you alter yourself for one woman (or group of persons), another woman or group may not like you, and you could go around in a vicious cycle trying to please people. It's totally pointless in the end. However, if someone you trust and respect critiques some aspect of you with good intention, feel free to judge (honestly) whether or not it is accurate – instead of dismissing the critique automatically or accepting it without questioning its authenticity.

Be honest and open: We're all imperfect, growing, learning human beings. If you feel ashamed or insecure about any aspect of yourself — and you feel that you have to hide those parts of you, whether physically or emotionally — then you have to come to terms with that and learn to convert your so-called self perceived flaws into individualistic grooves. Be honest with yourself, but don't beat yourself up; apply this philosophy to others, as well. There is a difference between being critical and being honest; learn to watch the way you say things to yourself and others when being honest. Remember that being honest does not mean you start discussing intimate details about your life with a girl you have just met. So use your common sense judgment.

Stop worrying about the outcome: Relax, just be yourself and enjoy the moment. So what if she does not like you? There are plenty of fish in the sea. What if you goof up? It is okay as long as you think it is. In fact it is a great attribute when a man knows how to laugh at his own mistakes. Girls would usually view this as an attractive quality.

Celebrate your individuality: Whether it's your sense of style, or even your manner of speaking, if your preferred way of doing something strays from the mainstream, then be proud of it...unless it's destructive to yourself or others. Be a character, not a stereotype.

Every day is different: Accept that some days you feel down, on some other days you're on the high. Girls or people you know may raise eyebrows and even make fun, but as long as you can shrug and say "Hey, that's just me" and leave it at that, people will ultimately respect you for it, and you'll respect yourself.

Believe in who you are: If you're always working to be someone you're not, you'll never be a happy person. Be yourself and show the world you're proud of the way you are! Nobody knows you better than you and that's how it should be. You deserve to be your own best friend, so start trying to figure out how you can be that. If you had to hang out with yourself for a day, what is the most fun type of person you could be, while still being yourself? What is the best version of you? Believe in this idea and use that as your starting point.

Follow your own style: The common thing a lot of men do is copy other people's actions because it seems like the better route to fit in, but really, shouldn't you stand out? Standing out yes, is very hard, but you need to try avoid assuming other people's perspectives of you. Maybe you like to sit outside on the deck under a umbrella in the middle of the rain, maybe you have different ideas of things, maybe you like strawberry cake instead of the common chocolate cake - whatever you are, accept it. Being unique in your own way is absolutely beautiful and it will attract more females to you than you can dream of.

2.10 What are the common mistakes men make when trying to be themselves?

There is a difference between being yourself and **being**

rude. Everyone has their own preferences and opinions. If you **disrespect women** who disagree with you, you will appear rude in social situations. Conversely, don't agree with something you honestly don't think is right. Just remember not to try to **force your opinions** on other people.

Be respectful of her opinion
Be aware of your place in this world
Try to **accommodate others** and you will be accepted by others
Try to grow as a better individual from within

As the famous song goes, "Life's not worth a darn until you can say, *I am what I am*." When you can sincerely say it, you will know that you can be yourself. An evolving authentic individual full of life and respectful of others. **This is what the women want**. They do not want a 'rude arrogant pig'. Being yourself can be cool. It can get females to notice you but don't overdo it. **Never** try to

mock people who are different than you, for all you know these women you are trying to impress could be making fun of you for the same reason!

2.11 How to overcome nerves when picking-up women?

Being nervous is natural but if it is going to stop you from picking-up women then it is not good for you. Here are some effective tips to overcome your nerves. Practice will make you perfect. **Be yourself. Imagine that you are talking to a friend.** That will relax the sexual tension and allow more comfortable conversation. Make **eye contact** while speaking to show that you are interested. (But don't stare or gaze!) Be **respectful** to women. They are not mere objects - always keep that in mind. **Compliment** the **little things**; the things that most men wouldn't notice. When you do that, you let her know that the little things she does don't go unnoticed, and makes her feel special. However please do not over compliment as it will make you look desperate. In fact under-do so that she keeps talking to you to see what else you have to say. Drop one complement here and there. **Practice** with a friend. A big barrier is the fear of rejection. Eliminate this factor by approaching and picking up a woman for your friend (but make sure your friend knows!). Since your own ego isn't at stake, you'll be less inhibited in your approach. You'll see it's no big deal and will want to pick up for yourself next time. Focus on baby steps. **Treat dating like a twelve-step program.** Start with a **smile**; show everyone (not just the cute women) you're friendly and approachable. On following days, move up to saying "hi." A few days after that, engage in small talk. Keep going as you gradually open yourself up to women and see it's not as hard as you thought. If you make a blunder, ignore it. Most women are more forgiving than you believe. If beautiful women intimidate you, take baby steps up the beauty scale. Start by approaching more average-looking women you feel confident with. As you become more at ease with them, move on to prettier women, and so on. Start by asking this special girl simple questions. You can show that you care by asking her how her day was. Learn to **listen**. Don't do all the talking. Let women talk about themselves for a while. Ask open-ended questions and just sit back and listen. If the conversation lulls, have new conversation topics ready. And to ease the burden of initiating something, have a few **icebreakers handy** to get the ball rolling. **Don't take things personally.** If you want to succeed in the game of romance, you can't take every comment, insinuation or joke that a woman might throw your way as a personal insult. **People sometimes say things they don't mean.** You'll have nothing to be self-conscious about if nothing bothers you. Talk to a lot of women. Don't be afraid to chat up everyone you meet, from the old lady doing her groceries to the bank teller. Practice makes perfect. **Get out and socialize.** Join activities in which you're always interacting with people, such as the gym, exercise classes, dance class, a college society, or a hobby club etc. In these environments, you must always socialize, and after a while, you'll get comfortable with it. Moreover, you're practically guaranteed to meet interesting women once you start going out. **Don't fear rejection**. Great boxers go in the ring knowing there's a chance they'll lose. Similarly, you can't expect to succeed every time. Nothing is hundred percent black or white. So view every encounter with a woman as a positive learning experience. Look for the grey areas. The trick here is to not be self-conscious. **Shyness and hesitation occur when you think about your flaws.** Instead, accept yourself as you are – no one is perfect, we are all mixture of good and bad. When meeting women focus your thoughts entirely on the woman you're talking to. You'll forget about your nerves and she'll be flattered by the attention and confidence. It starts with you. When you leave your shyness behind, which will take time and persistence, you'll see how much your life will change. You'll begin to go after what you want with fewer fears. Remember a *'great secret':* should you enter a room and feel those familiar nerves, remember that most people you meet are too busy worrying about what others think about them to really notice and judge you. And on top of everything, human memory is too short. So even if you fumble no one will remember it in a few days because everyone is busy with their own problems in life.

2.12 How to have good manners?

Good manners are important for creating good impression on women you meet. It involves display of **respect, care, and consideration** for others. We are all judged by the actions we take in front of others. Developing good manners is always a great idea for anyone looking to make a better impression. Here are some ideas to help you. Always try to **think before you speak** and **choose your words carefully** not to offend others. Being very loud can be considered rude in many social situations. Also avoid using crude humor based on offensive topics. Women may laugh at your jokes but that does not mean they are getting impressed. Show

courteous gestures like holding door open etc and also greet women respectfully. Show interest in what they have to say and **avoid belittling others or spreading gossips**. Always check your voice when speaking; speak in a **pleasant tone** and very clearly. Smile through your voice! **Express gratitude and thank** her when appropriate. Try to speak to her as you would like to be treated. Having manners is like the 'Golden Rule' of social behavior. Do not attempt to pick faults or correct others in social situations. One of the easiest ways to appear good mannered is to be silent and only talk when you have something important to say. This adds weight to your words. Always use the essentials like - pardon, thank you, please, you're welcome, my pleasure etc. However **don't be overly polite** with or you may come across as a weak, spineless, or needy. Remember having bad manners can often be associated with having poor character.

Section 3: Meeting Women

3.1 How to meet women?

Women everywhere are waiting to be asked out by men! The number of single women are on the rise. All you need is some know - how on **conversational and social skills** and a bit of **courage which comes with practice.** Here are few tips on how to deal with this issue. Make yourself **presentable** with a sense of style and proper self care. You never know when the opportunity comes by. If you feel you are too boring, put on something different /flamboyant that will make you stand out from the other guys and change your mood. If you think you're good enough for a woman, she will think you are, too. If you don't think you're good enough for her, then she probably won't think so, either. Hence, be relaxed and confident. This shows other women that you have good taste and that you're giving them a complement just by talking to them. **Never present yourself as needy.** Observe the guys that are getting attention from women at parties and watch the way they keep their interest. It is important to **learn by observing** how to engage a woman's interest and keep the conversation flowing, hence establishing common ground for conversation within a few minutes. Learn to **accept and ignore rejection.** Rejection is part of the game and being rejected doesn't necessarily mean there's something wrong with you. Repeated rejection, however, does mean there probably is something wrong with your approach that you need to change. Be graceful and never ashamed. **Always be on the prowl. Talk to women wherever you go.** It gives you practice and helps overcome the fear of talking to them. **Plan on where to hunt.** Smile and be friendly. **Make a connection with her.** Try and find out what this person really loves in the world, and let her tell you all of the things she loves about it. Then, tell her you feel just the same way about some things, but disagree with her opinions on other things. Make her get involved in a conversation. If your target is with a group of friends, make friends with her friends, so they do not think you are just some creep trying to get laid (especially if you are). Then, after you have sufficiently impressed the group, you can start to talk to the target woman. During conversation do not get nervous if there is a period of silence. **Remain confident** and search for other cues to continue the conversation. Borrow your cute niece or nephew and take them out to the store or mall. Women love a man who is looking after an adorable small **child!** Most women will smile and this is your cue to start a conversation. If your lifestyle allows, get a dog or preferably a **puppy**. Be aware that a dog may live for 10-15 years, and being a highly social animal, will need company and mental stimulation on a daily basis. Also be aware that puppies will become dogs. If you can't keep a dog, you're probably best off borrowing one to take to the park for a walk. **Work on your career**. As your success grows, so will your dating pool. Be patient and play the numbers game. Don't get discouraged by rejection. **Don't assume that good looking women are unapproachable.** A woman who is above average is probably sick of men hitting on her. A woman who is way above average, really stunning, probably doesn't get hit on as much. Rejection from a great-looking woman doesn't feel so bad. These women tend to be kinder and more gracious than women who are fed up with all the jerks. Know when to end the conversation. Always leave the conversation to be continued at a later date. **Do not exhaust the conversation** as things can turn awkward and she may lose interest. **Do not over analyze the situation**. Just make eye contact, smile, say hello, and start an innocent conversation with her just like you would with your guy friends. Offer her a chewing gum or mint. This can help build closeness. **Never utter the word 'girlfriend'.** She will become defensive immediately. A mobile phone can make it a lot easier to get a phone number by casually handing it to her after a successful conversation, she will be obliged to type in her phone number!

3.2 How to pick-up women randomly?

Women are always complaining that there are not enough single men. This is because they are weary of being single and **expect that men will start approaching them more often**. You need to help them now ! Stop waiting for some woman to be introduced to you by your aunt. Take things in your own hand. Here is the game plan which is used by those men who are good at picking-up girls. Once you set your eyes on a target woman, get close to her and **open with a neutral question** which has nothing to do with you. Something about the place or something you observe happening. Do your best to **appear comfortable**, and she'll feel comfortable too. Treat her normally almost like one of your male **friends.** Do not make the mistake of treating her any different. Keep up the small talk without asking too many personal questions. Just be casual, **witty and relaxed**. After a while, if you're having a good time and she is comfortable with you, **cut off** the conversation by saying that you need to go but would like to continue the conversation later. If she agrees then make the next move to get her **contact number.** If she says she doesn't want to give you her number, you can joke with her and say that you promise to only call her fifty times a day, but that's all. You could also just get her **email address**. **Practice** talking to women in general throughout your day – whether you find them attractive or not. As you get more practice, you will be surprised at how easy and comfortable you feel when approaching women. A lot of women don't like the idea of learning how to pick up women. They think it's cheap. They read about pick-up artists like this...but it doesn't have to always be that way. Those same women (if they're single) are waiting for the right man to sweep them off their feet...to charm them, and woo them and make them feel special and beautiful...and that's what you can do with this kind of information if you use it wisely. **Watch where your eyes are.** Do not stare at her chest, or keep glancing away. Try to look into her eyes, but not too intensely, which may make her feel nervous. Don't force anything. **Do not use**

routines that are not congruent with your image. Do not analyze too much when you get rejected. It is all a number game. That's life. Pick yourself up and try again. Most women want to attract you with **something besides looks**. If she's hot, do not try to complement her look. Instead try to **elicit her values or something personal** and then reward her with a statement which provokes interest in her. However, only **compliment her if you sense that she is already attracted to you.** Any earlier will come over as needy. Don't underestimate yourself by thinking that you're either destined to be good with women, or you aren't. This is a social skill anyone can learn with practice.

3.3 How to approach a woman in public settings?

There are single women everywhere. Many of them feel that men are not really approaching them. Here are few tips to help you approach women in public settings without seeming offensive. You may even meet your future wife standing at a bus stop. You have to **get out there** and approach them. They are not going to appear in front of you by magic if you do not go out looking for dates. When you enter a public place screen the crowd and **seek eye contact casually**. Once you establish eye contact next step is to **smile**. If she returns your smile then try to break the ice by asking some **neutral question**. Do not worry about what she is thinking, just be **polite and friendly**. Wait for her **response** and if she is friendly then continue further. Wait for the **signals** that she is interested: laughing (at your hilarious jokes), flicking her hair around, etc. If she makes any physical contact, like touching your arm while she laughs, it's a good sign. Take a hint if she's not interested. If she's busy, or if your comic genius is not being appreciated, then say, "It was great to meet you" and cut your losses. If you come on too strong, some women might feel threatened. Take it **small steps at a time**. If you think she is interested, **don't overdo it**: be brief, return to your own work and keep option for future communication open by saying, "Maybe we can have a chat later."

3.4 How to look approachable in front of women?

In any social situation there will inevitably be a lot of beautiful females that you would like to talk to. It can be quite easy to talk to a stranger when you are in any social event. This is because **people** who go to social events are generally **looking for company**. You may think of yourself as an interesting person, but still you are not able to make connection with others? May be it could be that you're sending out the wrong signals. No matter how confident you are, you must **look approachable** too. If you look intimidating or preoccupied, females will be disinclined to talk to you. Here's how to use your body language to look more **friendly and approachable**. Avoid folded arms as they act as a barrier between you and the world. Be aware of what your body is saying. We all speak with body language, and you don't have to actually say anything to communicate a message to others. Unfortunately, your body may not always say what you want it to. If your gestures and posture are saying that you are too busy or maybe that you want to be left alone, it's not likely people will approach you. Females are keen on reading body language for cues, so it's important to pay attention to **what cues you are displaying**. Remember they are also human beings and are just as afraid of rejection as you are (or may be more!) Open up your body language. When people are uncomfortable in any situation they have a tendency to display closed body language. Examples include folding your arms in front of you, hunching over, and positioning your body so that you're angled away from others. These signals imply that you'd rather be left alone. If you'd rather not be left alone, make sure you're displaying **open body language** by angling yourself toward other people, sitting or standing with an upright (but not stiff) posture, and uncrossing your arms. Use your eyes to connect with people. Your eyes are not only your window to the world, they're also other people's window into you. If you bury your head in a book, stare at the floor, or look up at the ceiling, you close that window. This is all good if you don't want to be bothered on your way to work, but if you want to look friendly and approachable don't be afraid to **make eye contact** with people. Use a warm and genuine smile to charm others. A genuine smile uses the whole face, especially the eyes. A **warm, inviting smile** can put anyone at ease. It also makes you look like you're having a great time, which makes people want to be around you. If you catch someone's eye, be sure to give a little smile, and be sure to smile often during small talk. It lets people know you appreciate talking to them. **Smile with your eyes**. When you do make eye contact with a woman, do not stare or glare. Instead, soften your eye expression and make your eyes "smile" or "twinkle" to show that you're friendly and interested in talking to the other person. **Beware of unconscious negative gestures.** If you really want to socialize and meet women you should be careful not to appear excessively nervous. Touching your hand to your face, especially putting it over your mouth, or, if you have a drink, holding your glass by your mouth can give people the impression that you're not interested in talking to her. Gestures, such as foot tapping, can signal impatience or boredom, so women may think you do not have time to talk or aren't interested in conversation. Other nervous habits like picking at your cuticles or biting your fingernails for instance — can also make you appear distant or lost in thought. Once again, just pay attention to what your body is saying, and you can avoid putting up these barriers. If your are in a social situation, **try to enjoy the moment**. Your body language usually communicates your deepest emotions at any given time. So the best way to look approachable, then, is to actually enjoy yourself in social interactions. **Dress to suit your persona.** Your dress forms part of your appearance and can affect how approachable you look. Dressing in light/bright colors with textures that look soft to the touch will make you stand out more in a crowd and look more approachable to females. Position yourself comfortably. If you're standing up, but the other person is sitting down (or vice verse) people may find it difficult and somewhat awkward to talk to you. If you want to talk to someone, or if you're already talking with someone, position yourself so that you can **comfortably talk to her.** Also do not gauge her interest level based solely on how approachable or unapproachable she appears. The person may not realize what her body language conveys.

3.4 How to have a happy face?

Our face is the mirror of our mind. It is important to have a happy smiling face when you are meeting any woman. Honestly who would like a grumpy person! A warm smile would project the warmth in your personality. You can improve your face value hundred times when you learn to smile with warmth and emotions in it. Women are driven by emotions more than anything else. Here are some tips for you to try. Look in the mirror to **study your smile**. Friendly faces are usually **well-hydrated and clean**. Brush your teeth often, and make yourself look approachable. Notice what makes you happy and smile. Think of those things often, but try not to have a too dreamy look. **Relax** your face muscles. When you're stressed, your eyebrows tend to furrow up, and that makes you look as if you are too stressed or deep in thought for someone to approach you. Learn to smile often. Make it look genuine, especially around the eyes. Make eye contact with females you would like to meet. Make your eyes seem bright and alert. **Try to be a happy person in general, not complaining much about life.** Rather enjoying it as it comes – because you are wise to know that life is short. Make the women think of you as an **optimistic person**. Always focus on the bright side of everything when you talk to them. No one likes a whinging miserable person.

3.5 How to draw attention of women?

In order to overcome being single, it is important to increase your chances of interactions with women.

Wherever it is, and whoever it is that you wish to attract, there's a lot that you can do to increase your chances out there. There are a number of things you can work on to increase your chances of success with women. Meet other people by **going out**. If you stay within the four walls of your home nothing will change. Dress nicely and make yourself **presentable** to others. Looking good often means feeling good and that definitely pays off. Be **culturally aware and an interesting person** by knowing a little bit of common current topics to help with **conversation**. Truly knowing about the things that really interest you will genuinely make you a more interesting person. Be able to put in your own views during conversation. Develop your own style. **Uniqueness** is crucial because it is what differentiates you in the sea of "other fish" in the eyes of women. **Mirror her actions and body language** subtly without being obvious. This not only shows them that you are flattered with them, it also shows that you are noticing their actions. **Flirt** physically. Casual touches are a great way to gauze the direction of things. If the other person seems comfortable with you touching their hand or brushing their arm, then you have a good litmus test for their response. Make eye contact. Look into the other person's eyes when talking. The eyes have been called the window to the soul. Genuinely appreciate the other person though your looks. Do not be afraid to **exchange contact details** like phone numbers, email addresses, etc. if the person seems interested. They may find it more stimulating to see your courage!

3.6 How to act around women?

Interacting with women can become less intimidating for most men if they follow the principles given below. Gradually with practice it will become easier and enjoyable. Firstly, always **be yourself**. Avoid trying to project an alternate personality to attract women. It will be more stressful for you. Instead be your true self and develop on your personality and social skills. Any woman that does not appreciate you for who you are does not deserve your attention. **Relax and be calm**. It is okay to make mistakes as you are a human being. Do accept this as a part of life and **do not think of previous sour experiences**. Every moment is a new opportunity and as they say the past does not equal the future. **Respect** all women equally. Irrespective of whether you find the woman attractive or not, treat her with respect. Do not ignore or demean women. **Avoid comparing** women with one another and do not talk about past relations. Exhibit **good manners**. Be polite and courteous. Avoid sexist or racist comments and refrain from swearing or saying offensive things about others. Saying things that you know would probably offend some people isn't a good way to make or keep friends. If you **act like a decent man** who is respectful of other people in general, women will be more likely to welcome your company. Make eye contact and make her laugh. It's okay to tease women a little, but generally not about her appearance. Also if you're not sure that she will take your teasing the right way, try to avoid it. Physical contact depends on the closeness of your relationship. **Be sensitive to her feelings** about it. Initially keep it minimal before she gets to know you. **Women like to be made special**. Sincere and honest compliments are good but use them selectively. However only say things which are very personal if you obviously know her well and want to move beyond flirting. **Don't panic if you do something embarrassing.** A lot of women find that really cute. **Use humor to recover from the goof up** – it will make you cool. **Assess her body language** to read how comfortable she is with you. Notice when you're having a conversation and she seems uncomfortable, change the subject. Watch her movements, if she's shifting her weight a lot and not making eye contact, chances are she's uncomfortable. Be friends with her and get to know her friends as well. This will show her that you're pleasant and friendly person. Be the same around her and her friends. There is nothing wrong with trying to make her feel special long into a relationship, but trying to 'kiss-up' to her, especially within the first few weeks of knowing her, will do more harm than good, and you will be labeled more as a friend who tries to buy her attention than a potential mate. Initially **don't try too hard** to sell yourself. You will lose her interest. **Never tell any of your friends** what happens between you unless it is a really close and trustworthy friend.

3.7 How to get to know someone while remaining Mysterious yourself?

It can be more attractive to women if you **do not reveal everything** about yourself as soon as you meet. Wait till you get close to her. Because being too open about yourself with the wrong people decreases your importance to them. Here's how you can proceed! Be a good listener and **let her do the talking. Ask intelligent questions** to stimulate her interest. Asking questions will put a train of thoughts into your conversation partner's head. If you follow it in a clever manner (and the person enjoy talking in general), she will not notice that they never got around to asking "So, what about you?". If they do notice it, chances are it's already gotten pretty late and you can say "I'll tell you next time." This way, you already have a reason to meet her again. Evaluate every situation according to the merits of it. Talk about **general stuff** and keep her interest going during the conversation and slowly reveal about yourself. If you do choose to share something about yourself, **be honest**. If that person and you just click, **don't be too reserved**. It might ruin something really great.

Section 4 : Understanding Women

4.1 What creates attraction in women?

There are a lot of misconceptions about what creates attraction in women. Although there is no standard set of rules however relationship research has shown that you do not need to have huge muscles, a lot of confidence, a cool car or be a jerk. On the contrary all scientific research shows that none of those things are absolutely essential. Different women can have different preferences. However here are a list of things which usually work with most women. Firstly, be **pleasant** and **courteous**. There's nothing sweeter to a woman than a **genuinely kind man**. Have **manners** and act **caring**. Use your niceness correctly. Being nice doesn't mean you have to be timid, spineless and a pushover. You have to be **confident** in yourself. But this is where you have to draw the line between confident-and-courteous and over-confident-and-a-jerk. Care about people. **Don't be mean** or ill-wish others. When speaking to women, **appear interested** in what they're saying. Say kind things, especially if you're talking about your ex-anything. Making humiliating fun of people is extremely unattractive. Be **honest** with her. Nothing is attractive about lies. If you really want to be with her, always tell the truth and never twist stories. If you're only looking for a one-time thing and not a relationship, do not give her false hope. Nothing is worse than a lying jerk. Have a sense of **humor**. However avoid racist or politically incorrect jokes. Be confident under your own skin. Show that you want a **commitment** towards the woman. **Appreciate** life and your future and it may be given back to you. Have eye contact. Always look into her eyes and don't disconnect before she does. It proves your self-confidence. Be yourself. Remember that different types of women like different types of men. Just because one woman is not interested in you, doesn't mean that others wont be. Some women may like jerks, some may like athletes, others are into loners. So don't try to be someone you're not. Not all women want the same things in men. Just be and show your **true self**. Give them that which they do not have. A woman with a "great personality" probably doesn't hear about how beautiful her eyes are that often, whereas a drop dead gorgeous woman may hardly be respected enough to be asked what her political views on a topic are. Know your audience, and adapt. If they are used to what you are saying, what do you think would gives you the advantage over the next guy? **Notice** the silly, most minute **details** in her. It shows you care enough to notice and gives you a good opener in a conversation. Remembering some small detail about something she said, dropped into a conversation later is always a winning move!

4.2 How to read a woman's body language?

Eighty percent of our communication is through our body language. So learning to read female body language can put you ahead of other competitors. Here is a list of some of the common subconscious body language clues of interest that a woman may show.

Her lips: Big smiles, relaxed face, biting / licking / wetting her lips, protrusion of lips

Her eyes: Gazes in your eyes with deep interest, wide pupils, regular eye contact, exaggerated raising of eyebrows, winking, frequent blinking, fluttering of eyelashes, smiling with eyes

Her hair: Fingers through hair, twirls her hair, throws hair backward repeatedly.

Her clothing: Wearing clothes that are provocative or exposing, or she is repeatedly fixing, patting or smoothing her outfit to make herself look better.

While she is seated: She moves in time to the music, with her eyes on you, starts sitting straight up and her muscles appear to be firm, sitting with her legs open, legs crossed in a manner to reveal her thigh, legs are rubbing against each other, legs are rubbing against the leg of the table, her crossed leg is pointed towards you or if that same leg is rocking back and forth towards you.

Her hands: She exposes the palms of her hand facing you, she rests an elbow in the palm of one hand, while holding out her other hand, palm up, rubs her wrists up and down, one hand touching one of her breasts, rubs her chin or touches her cheek, fondling keys, sliding hands up and down a glass, playing with toys or other things on the table, plays with her jewelry, especially with stroking and pulling motions, touches your arm, shoulder, thigh, or hand while talking to you.

Her voice: She raises or lowers the volume of her voice to match yours, speeds up or slows down her speaking to match yours, laughs in unison with you, in a crowd she speaks only to you and focuses all of her undivided attention on you.

Miscellaneous: She mirrors your body language and body positions, blushes while being around you, leans over and speaks into her friend's ear, just like in junior high school, stands with her head cocked slightly at an angle, one foot behind the other, hips slightly thrust forward. At a party - she seems to appear frequently in your vicinity and if you move to another spot, soon she appears again, you catch her glancing in your direction, she bumps into you… accidentally, touches you... etc.

When talking to a girl, these are some of the other important signs to watch for: Keep the conversation going with small talk, letting her do most of the talking, so she'll think you're a good listener. Watch her reaction to friendly touching, or does she touch you, however if you make advance and she's not looking for that, things may not end well. Does she laugh at your jokes / humor. Does she turns away quickly when you turn to her direction, this can be a negative sign, or may be she just doesn't want you to catch her looking at you. Many women are offended by men checking them out in a distasteful way! Most females will take offense when she notices that your eyes are wavering (especially on the very first date). Try to resist the temptation!

Note of caution: Not all women have the same body

language, also it may be influenced by culture or social upbringing. Also not all women can correspond well, may be due to shyness or lack of   self confidence.

4.3 How to know if a woman likes you?

If you have a intuitive feeling that she likes you but you are not sure, then follow these steps and find out if she really likes you. Strike up a small conversation and **observe her reactions**. Is she laughing or giggling, is her adjusting her hair or clothes? Watch for signs of **flirting**. Also if she likes you, she will probably **laugh** at all your jokes even if they're not funny. Notice if she **touches** you more often than what friends do. Observe how she **looks at you.** If she likes you, she will either hold it for a long time or pull away immediately if she is shy. Either of these could mean that she likes you. Look for her eyes to light up when she sees you or hears your name. Look at her **friends**. If you see most of her friends glancing back at you and smiling or giggling, this means that she is telling her friends about you. Look out for the '**damsel in distress' sign**. Sometimes a woman will pretend to be really bad at something, and say that they can't do it. That is your cue to offer some assistance, and she will most likely be doing this on purpose just to see your reaction. **Never directly ask** her if she likes you. This tends to backfire if said improperly because the girl will get all tense and uncomfortable.

4.4 How to attract a woman older than you?

If you are attracted to a woman older than you, it can become a problem for you unless you **prepare** yourself to deal with the situation. Make **friends with her friends** first. That way, you don't look like a complete outsider and it makes you look (and feel) more connected with the group. Join an activity she is in and/or might be interested in. Attracting an older woman requires the exact **same skills** as getting a woman your age; you just have to be better at them. Try to be **mature** in your conversation, avoid sweet-talk and talk about **intelligent topics**. Talk about things which women of her age think as appropriate. However when you do talk to her, don't try to sound smarter than you would normally be at your age, it may make you look like an idiot. Be aware that she might like you but she might have a problem dating a younger guy because her friends might make fun of her.

4.5 How to get an uninterested woman to fall for you?

Sometimes you may be faced with a situation where you know the woman or maybe you're even friends with the woman, and even though you're crushing pretty hard, you don't think she feels the same way. Here's how to steal her heart before someone else does. Start acting more **caring** and **interested** in her. Use **comforting words** and be interested in how she's **feeling** and how her life is going. That means ask her how her day's been or what's wrong if she's upset, side with her if she's upset about something and **listen** when she talks to you.

Complement her intelligence, talents or quirks. Recognize that girls love big gestures of **affection**. You may attempt one of these after you've displayed the above and are starting to feel a little closer in the relationship. Be **creative**. Try sweet gestures like sending her flowers as a surprise etc. If all else fails, remember that you can't force someone to like you and maybe its not meant to be. If it really is meant to be, now is not the right time and there will be a time for you to be with her later in life. Do not obsessively ask her what is wrong, she will find this annoying after a while. Don't over compliment, she will find this creepy and wonder what's gotten into you. Only make a big gesture of affection if you are confident that she is accepting the new phase of the relationship. **Never** comment about someone in an **unkind** way in front of her. She'll think you do that to everyone.

4.6 How to learn the Art of Seduction?

In order to learn the Art of Seduction, you must learn to

play with her mind. Make her feel so **comfortable** with you that she **keeps thinking about you** even when you are not there. **Listen** and remember what she talked about. **Find out** her likes and dislikes, her needs and desires, her insecurities, her strengths, her secrets - all this will help you build up trust and she will start to feel closer to you. **Talk** to her frequently. The best approach is **email**. It gives you direct access to her head because you can be as intimate as you want and she can go over your words while you are not around. Listen to her using not just your auditory senses, but using your other senses as well. A woman communicates by using more than mere words. Usually, she speaks with **body language**, eyes, and sometimes even through touch. **Laugh** with her and agree with her when you can. Be slow with your approach and be **patient**. Your ability to **resist her** will make her wonder if you're really interested, and will motivate her to show you that she's worth being interested in. **Kiss with** your **eyes** first. Women need to feel a deeper emotional connection with you. You begin this connection through your words and then your eyes. Increase the physical intimacy slowly. Begin touching a woman with simple hugs, pats on the back, etc. Then gradually increase it by bringing her in closer...kiss with your eyes. Then move on to simple kisses (pecks). Again, take it slow. Talk about sex or sexy things. At some point, begin to talk about sex...not between the two of you, but general experiences you've had. Once you inject the topic of sex, it will be on their mind when they think about you. With women, it's all about **familiarity and safety**. Talking about the act makes them more comfortable with the act. Tell a woman you want her in a **tender** way. Watch her reaction. If she is ready, then plan on setting up the situation for it to happen. When it's the right time, always ask for permission ("Are you okay, darling?") and be ready to back off at any time if she is not ready. **Respect** the woman at all times.

4.7 How to Seduce a Woman?

Attraction and seduction are not the same. While attraction is passive, seduction is **active influence** by using **manipulative** strategy. It involves the art of distracting a woman from all of your shortcomings and making her fall in love with you for who you are – this is called seduction. Here are few tips to get you going on the right track. Create a **charming** positive image with **everyone** you meet. Manage your **reputation** with all. Show that you have pleasant, charming and friendly **personality**. Try to be **different** to the regular guy in your approach to women in order to create curiosity in her. Be **patient** in your approach and look for hints from her. Talk about your preference for **pleasurable** things and for things that she likes. Create a sense of **surprise** in her by tiny caring gestures. **Write** to her whenever you plan to give her a small gift. Use ambiguous physical contact. **Empathy** is important to establish an emotional connection which is essential to seduction. Reveal yourself slowly and only when directly asked. Don't show more of yourself than she asks for. When the mystery is gone, the seduction is over. Show your **strengths** but never boast about yourself directly. Physically attractive seducers will be able to seduce much faster than unattractive ones, because the attraction is already there. However, unappealing men will have an easier time getting close to girls and gaining **access** to their **hopes and dreams**. Go slow and do not let her sense that you are seducing her. Seducing a woman is like dancing with a woman. **Never** be too possessive or **controlling**. Seducing women takes a lot of trial and error. Don't be discouraged with failure. Study the biographies, writings and speeches of the world's greatest seducers: Erroll Flynn, Casanova, Lord Byron, Charles De Gaulle, Gabriele D'Annunzio, etc.

4.8 How to seduce an older woman?

Learning how to seduce older woman can be fun and creative. You need to use slightly different techniques. Try to know her as a person and behave accordingly.

Always try to behave in a **sophisticated and mature manner** to be successful in your mission. Concentrate on her best qualities when you are around her. **Appreciate** her for who she is. Let her know why you are attracted to her. **Ignore her negative points**. If they sense you have a problem with their age they may lose interest in you. When you take her out, choose a place where you both will be comfortable and the two of you will have fun. Older women are **independent** and appreciate men who are **not needy** and dependent. They want to feel that you are capable of dealing with the complexities of life. You should try to project a **confident** image in front of mature women. Be **honest** and open with her (even if you want to take her to bed).

4.9 How to treat a woman well?

Every woman wants to be **acknowledged** and **appreciated**. Be **compassionate** and **understanding** of her emotional needs. **Respect her future** plans. **Let her**

talk about herself. They want to be able to discuss future plans and problems they might be having, without difficulties. They want a person with whom they can **relate and trust**. Reflect her feelings so that she knows you really heard her. **Complement** her from time to time and **make her feel relaxed**. However avoid the temptation to worship her or put her on a pedestal. She is as human as you are, and the more willing you are to accept that, the less likely she is to disappoint you. Look at her and **smile** lovingly. Most women long for **romance** in their lives. Think creatively and let your true **affections** show. Nothing speaks more than **written words**. Overall be **courteous** to her and make her feel at ease with you.

4.10 How to be an irresistible man?

Here are few ingredients for success. To be an irresistible guy you need to be **pleasant** and **gracious** to women even if you don't know them. It's also a great idea to be a

gentleman to your and **her family** as well, as both sides can greatly impact a woman's view of yourself. **Respect all women**, ugly or not, and never be mean to them, no one likes a mean guy. Be brave and always offer a shoulder to cry on. Be **sensitive** and **understanding**. This is what most girls see once they begin to spend more than five minutes with you, and it's more important than looks. Be **dignified** and **confident** and learn to **comfort** women when they are hurt. When talking to her ask questions and **listen** carefully to the answers. **Never insult** her about her looks or her interests. Be sensitive and just listen, most women really love this. Don't show that you think she is a sex object – many girls do not like it. **Don't talk** about your **ex, or compare** her with others. **Defend** her against other people who try to bring her down but do not be overprotective. Give her **own space** when she is sad. However try to figure out if you can help her in any way. Try to pretend you don't notice when she does something wrong. **Pamper** her in small ways when possible. Show you care for her when she is sick, walk her home –

display little day to day caring gestures. She will love you for all this **attention**.

4.11 How to win trust of a woman?

Getting close to a woman depends on winning her trust. Generally speaking for building trust you need to be **honest** and just be yourself. **Do not boast**, this can be a really big conversation disaster. Be careful about talking for too long about the same thing. **Never tell obvious lies** to her. If she talks about a problem or something that bothers her, **pay attention and listen actively**. Ask **follow up questions** in order to try to make her see the problem from different perspectives. Generally when ladies speak about a problem, it is because they want to ease the burden from their shoulders instead of solving it (unless they explicitly say so, of course). Show her that you are **always there for her**, this will tell her you are reliable. **Keep secrets**. Try to be **humorous**, this makes most women more relaxed. **Do what you say**. Volunteer

information about yourself to her to prove that you have nothing to hide. Best not to omit important details because it is hard to keep up with a string of omissions. She will start to notice contradictions in your stories and you will be considered a liar, even if you are only omitting a little! Don't mask truths. If you do lie, admit to it.

4.12 How to act caring?

Women like men who **care** for them and **adores** them. It is the key emotional need of most women. Here are some tips to help you. **Accept her** and **cherish her** for who she is. Pay enough **attention** to her so that she does not feel like taken for granted. Call her when you guys are not together and tell her that you are thinking about her. Be **protective**, but not overprotective. Make her feel as if you would do anything to make sure she is safe. You may say to her "I just don't want you to get hurt." Be sweet, but also courageous. Girls absolutely love a guy who is sweet but can be the hero that saves her life. Put your arm around her waist, not around her shoulder. It's more **romantic**. Women like it when you are comfortable around them. Don't get annoyed when she wants you to meet all her friends, keep your arms on her (it will make her feel secure). Be the first to kiss her. **Flirt** with her all the time, but don't be annoying. If she seems to be getting irritated when you do it, it's the sign to stop. Be confident and brave. Even if you do your best, life happens differently at times. So don't put yourself down if you were always there for her but she ended the relationship over more complicated reasons.

4.13 How to make her happy when she is feeling down?

When your target woman is feeling down, here are some ways to influence her by making her feel better. Listen to her with **empathy**. Try to understand her thoughts and **be in her shoes**. Just listen and let her vent her frustration.

You need not try to provide any suggestions. Let her get it off her chest. This shows you care and love her. **Just be there.** When appropriate let them know that you are there to help if needed. Give her a **comforting hug**! Tell her how you feel about them. She would appreciate knowing that she is appreciated as an individual! Say anything sweet you truly mean, but have always kept on the inside. It'll **make her smile** physically and mentally, knowing that it came from the bottom of your heart. Try to **avoid** making comments about how you **pity** her. However if she wants to be alone, leave her alone, but let her know that if she changes her mind and wants to talk, you're willing to hear whatever she has to say. Also don't try too hard to cheer her up! Just be understanding and sensitive to her emotional state.

Section 5: Talking to Women

5.1 How to talk to a woman for the first time?

Women like to be treated with tenderness. So please be kind, gentle and thoughtful in your approach. Here is a structure which can help you deal with this situation. Try to appear **confident** and **carefree**. Be **funny** in your conversation and have a smile on your dial. Don't give up you if you feel nervous, because it is okay to be nervous and you will be able to overcome your nervousness with **practice**. If you feel nervous, you can actually tell her that and also give reasons (what and why?) If you get scared take a deep breath. **Compliment** her with something that is true, this will make her feel comfortable with you. Just keep it to one because if you overdo she will freak out. Make sure that your sense of humor is not offensive to her, otherwise it will backfire. Make her feel at home by talking openly and honestly. **Refrain** from saying things which may appear **sexually provocative** when you meet her for the first time. Explore non-controversial grounds of mutual interest for conversation. Show interest in what she is saying by asking questions but make sure you do not appear to be too intrusive. Let the conversion flow naturally. Do not try too hard. It will come **naturally** with practice! Give her your phone number, MySpace, Facebook, etc. when you know each other well enough. As a last tip, try not to act desperate! Acting desperate may freak her out. Remember this: Do not just come out and openly say that you like her because that would put her in an awkward position and the results might not be what you want them to be. If you don't think she will like you, still try because just talking to her casually after a while might make her change her mind about you once she gets comfortable with you. **Never** say anything disrespectful which will **make her feel bad**.

5.2 How can you tell if a woman is not interested in you?

Since dating is a number game, it is important to realize quickly which woman is not interested in you. This will help you to move on quickly without wasting your valuable time. Here are few common indicators to guide you. When you call her she will be **extremely quiet**, or **wouldn't ask any questions**, or would make an **excuse to hang up**. Whenever you two talk face to face she will **look away**. Whenever you ask her to hangout or suggest that you two do something together, she'll say - can I think about it or I am **busy** that day. She is **hesitant** about giving her number. She flirts but that's how she is with everyone. She says she'll call but after about a week she still **hasn't called**. She sees you and **ignores** you or walks away. She seems to be always listening to what you have to say. She **doesn't ask** anything about you. You **heard** she's interested in someone else. Always remember: 'There are plenty of fish in the sea'.

5.3 How to ask a woman out?

Asking a woman out is not always an easy feat, but it is doable if you have a plan for it. Read these guidelines, draw some courage, and ask her out! Once you have built up a **rapport** with the woman, judge her level of interest from her eye contact, smiling, laughter, and enthusiasm in her responses. Read her body language. **Observe** how she looks at you. If she likes you, she will either hold it for a long time or pull away immediately. Either of these could mean that she likes you. If she pulls away quickly, it could mean she is nervous but she still likes you. **Pop the question casually**. "Hey, why don't you come to the movies with me this weekend?" (It doesn't have to be the movies - it can be anything you're interested in, and that you think she'll enjoy too.) Another good way to ask is "I heard about this movie, _____. What do you think about it?" If she says she'd like to see it, ask if she'd want to see it with you. If she says "As in a date?", don't be afraid to say yes. If she doesn't say that, just make a time, turn up and treat it like a date and she'll get the drift.

Keep your cool if she says no. Respond gracefully, like "No problem! Maybe another time. I'll see you around, OK?" And go about your business - there are other fish in the sea! Ask her **privately** when no other people are around. Having others around you will stir pressure on her to say yes or no. Ask her out **directly**. Instead of texting, getting other people to ask her out for you, or beating around the bush, just ask her. Even if you're nervous, this will increase your chances. Most women will admire your confidence if you are not arrogant about it. Don't be afraid of rejection! Most women have big hearts and will not let you down very easily, if at all. Some women agree to one date just because you asked and they're being nice. Don't take it the wrong way, it simply means she likes you enough to not hurt your feelings but not enough that she's ready for a relationship. The worst thing you can do before asking a girl out is not even having a friendship with her! When you do approach the girl, try not to start the conversation by a "Hey, can I talk to you?" or a "Can I ask you something?". Don't ask her out randomly, but these lines are giant hints that you are about to ask her out. This would be awkward. Instead blend it into the **conversation** as naturally as possible. If she says no, just ask "Oh, okay. Is it fine if we're still friends?" If you have to ask her out through a friend, you will get a "no" by default. Women do not enjoy hearing, "Hey! I'm asking you out for (Name of guy). He doesn't like you enough to overcome his lack of confidence." They are likely to hear this regardless of how tactful your friend is, unless her friend is a very close friend to both you and herself. Be **persistent**, but not too persistent. If she turns you down gently, then she's politely telling you she's not interested. If she flat out refuses, back away. You don't want any woman to think you're a stalker.

5.4 How to ask a woman out if she is already dating?

When you meet a woman that you enjoy talking to, and feel compatible with, it is only natural to want to ask her out. When you feel that she also is comfortable with you as well, and you sense vibes between you, you're bound to be encouraged. But when you find out that she's already seeing someone else, it can be hard to know what the next step is - and the best thing to do is **go for it**, and see what she says! **Express** your interest. Maybe in a phone call or an ordinary conversation, let her know you're interested by asking her over to watch a movie she's into or asking her out for a drink. Let her know that you know she's dating someone else, and that it doesn't have to be serious between you right now. Appreciate your **friendship**. Tell her that whatever she decides, your friendship doesn't have to change. Be interested in how she feels about the situation. If she's comfortable with it, discuss gradually how she feels about her current relationship. **Discuss her views** on relationships and dating, and ask her how she feels about dating more than one person at once. This should help you to find out where you stand, and it'll also help you to get to know her better. Be **prepared for rejection**. Realistically, if she's already seeing someone else then there's a chance she'll turn you down. If things don't go so well, that's cool. There are other women out there. She may seem like "the one", but there are many others that will make you feel the same way. Don't push it too much if she tells you she is already serious about the person she's seeing. If you persist, she might just find you annoying. Also some boyfriends might feel uncomfortable with you flirting with their girlfriend - be careful! In any case asking a woman out if she's already seeing someone and you know for a fact that she is not in an open relationship does have the chance of not only getting a kick to the teeth, but also losing her friendship.

5.5 How to ask a woman out if you are shy?

If you are shy, you are not alone. A a lot of women, even if they are pretty, have low self-esteem. Women over-analyze way more than men, and can take even the smallest thing in a bad way. If you are shy, just remember that any woman will be **flattered** just by you showing interest. First build up a **rapport** with her. **Observe** her body language. Then when you have broken **past her defenses**, ask her directly in a **causal friendly** way to join you for some activity. Avoid having anyone with you as it may make you feel more nervous. Just do it. **Do not hesitate** as you will more than likely back out. Unless you ask, you will never know.

5.6 How to ask a woman if she is single?

In life sometimes you may come across someone you really like without knowing much about her relationship stratus. Before you decide to hit on them, it is wise to find out if they are single. First get **acquainted** with her in a **friendly** manner. Then politely ask her the personal question. You can also use humor to ask her nicely. If she is already in a relationship, better to not get disappointed. Do not waste time to convince her to change her mind. Instead just move on. You can find lots of people like your "soul mate". Avoid obsessing over them, avoid flirting inappropriately and do not persist to ask them about their love life! If they say "No", you are done! No is no, no matter what you think. Just use your sense of **humor** and move on.

5.7 How to ask for her Phone Number?

When you meet someone you would like to see again, it is important to ask for her phone number. Here is an approach which can work in most cases. First start a **friendly conversation** with her. Example, "Hi Jane! How have you been?" If you don't know them, ask someone you know for an introduction. Just be yourself. A compliment is always a nice way to lead into a chat. Be honest though. Keep the conversation brief. You don't want to monopolize their time. **Wind up** the conversation by saying the following: "Hey, I don't want to hold you up. Can I call you sometime and we can chat more?" If the person urges you to stay and talk longer, then do so at their request. **Don't end** the conversation, get their **number first**. Call them in a few days, even if you just leave a message saying "Hi, I just wanted to say how nice it was to see you the other day, and I'm looking forward to seeing you again. I'll try you again, or please feel free to call me." Make sure you leave your name and phone number. Keep smiling in the event of a rejection, and say "OK, well here, I'll give you mine. I'd love to hear from you again." Give them your number and name written neatly on something noticeable. Don't use a torn scrap of receipt from your wallet. Go for it - you will never have any success if you don't try. Don't ask more than once, and leave them alone if they say no.

5.8 How to avoid talking about the same old things?

When you are meeting someone you have a crush on, it is important to sound interesting. The more knowledge you possess and varied your interests, the more different subjects you will be interested in talking about. Consider what your **common interests** are with this person? Do you like the same music? Don't know what music they like? Ask them! Having stuff in common is the reason most people become friends. Search for **new perspectives** in your own interests. **Study the reaction** of women you normally talk with when you try to bring up new topics. Remember, with exception to offensive language or culturally taboo subjects, there are **limitless possibilities**. Movies, music, fashion, business, sports, politics, celebrities, school, and current events, food even... the weather, offer unlimited conversational subjects, if you take a little time to be interested in them. Being creative is something people like to see in other people. Think of your own topics. When the group is talking about one subject, don't try to force a change in topic. Spend time **listening to others**, otherwise you will soon find few people willing to listen to you. Avoid talking **repetitively** about one or two topics only. Using **humor** in any conversation will make you likable and respectable and enable you to further the true essence of your mission with her as well!

5.9 How to have a great Conversation with women?

The art of conversation with women is not hard, but it takes practice. Conversation is a key to any woman's heart. Here are few tips which can impress her. Pay **attention** to what she is saying and **use her name. Allow her** to do most of the talking. Note her areas of **interest.** Ask appropriate **questions. Compliment** her sincerely to make her feel good about herself. Try **not to argue** or appear hostile. However sometimes exploring opposite points of view may encourage her to speak more. Do not panic over lulls. If the topic seems to have run out, use the pause to think for a moment and identify another conversation topic or question. Know when the conversation is over. Even the best conversations will eventually run out of steam or be ended by an interruption. Smile if you're leaving, and tell her you can't wait to talk to her again soon. **Ending on a positive note** will leave a good impression. Make a good first and last impression. Smile, ask open ended questions that require more than a yes/no answer, and really listen to the answers. Maintain eye contact and be as **friendly and polite** as possible. Don't be worried about the conversation and where it will go. Try to lead her into funny personal stories and anecdotes. However choose carefully when asking personal questions. You do not want to venture into overly personal issues. Always **think before you speak** and avoid politically incorrect topics. Let her finish her thoughts and then continue on with thoughts of your own. Remember that sometimes if a conversation isn't going well, it might not be your fault! Sometimes the other person is distracted / lost in thought, isn't willing to contribute, or is having a bad day. If they don't speak or listen, then they are the ones not using good conversation skills, not you.

5.10 How to come up with good conversation topics?

It is important to choose what you are talking about in front of women you have just met. This can **influence their opinion** about you. Some topics are inappropriate in some situations, and some are just plain boring. Here are some topics to keep the conversation alive. If you use **complimenting** as a way of initiating conversations, mention something **they did and then ask her how they did it**. There is no point in complementing her looks as then she may say thank you and the conversation will end. Another **harmless topic** can be the persons family and their siblings. However relations with parents and children can sometimes be more complicated and unpleasant. So stick with only issues comfortable to her. Other **neutral areas** of conversation are travel, food and drink, work, interest and hobbies. **Current events** are okay but stay away from political issues. Stay away from topics involving past relationships political or religious issues, job miseries, health problems, negative judgments or other issues which can be potentially inflammatory.

5.11 How to communicate positively with body language?

Body language must be **in tune with the words** you speak. Otherwise when you speak with any woman, she will not believe what you say. Be **natural and honest** and say what you mean. For most people, appropriate body language - that is, body language that effectively reinforces the speaker's meaning comes naturally when they mean what they say. If your **non-verbal signals** match your words, you'll not only communicate more clearly, you'll also be perceived as being more charismatic. Direct the most positive **gestures** toward the listener and negative gestures away from her. **Tone** of voice and inflection, although audible, are great indicators of meaning. However the actual tones used between people may not be accurately interpreted by the listener. Be careful to not misinterpret another person's tone of voice. When you are talking to women make sure your body language is **not withdrawn and insecure**.

Observe your own expressions and be mindful of what body language signals you send out to her, even if it's unintentional.

Section 6 : Dating

6.1 How to be calm on a first date?

First date can be stressful depending on how serious you are over the person. However it is important to **prepare yourself mentally** so that you can minimize your stress levels and maximize your confidence. **Don't have too many expectations**. Go into it with an **open mind**! Most first dates range from awkward to mediocre. There's no such thing as the perfect one. **Treat your date as if they're an old friend. Do not think of her as a stranger,** this can only make you more nervous. Playfully tease her as you might your friends, tell silly stories, don't be afraid to show off the person you are day-to-day. **Don't be phony** or pretend to be something / someone you're not. You don't want to start off with dishonesty if you have long term plans. Based on what you want in the future with this person, you can decide what topics of conversation you're comfortable with, what information about yourself you'd like to share, and what vibe to give off to them. Pick a date location that you'll feel **comfortable** in. Choose a **fun activity**; something that is different. Everyone goes to dinner and a movie! Do something different. For example, go shopping (window or regular), work out together, go to a bookstore and look around, etc. Choose an activity both of you can enjoy and are interested in. Often by doing these things you **show off your personality** most. **Dress and groom** yourself in a manner that's comfortable for you. If you don't feel like yourself, you'll be uneasy, and your date will be able to tell. Most first dates are really awkward, it's not until the second, third or however many that you really get comfortable. Just remember that your date is probably just as nervous as you are. **Be yourself** and **enjoy the experience** without stressing too much about the future.

<u>6.2 How to break the ice on the first date?</u>

You have to get yourself in the right mindset before you

go on your first date. You can minimize your anxiety by **preparing** yourself ahead of time with **conversation starters**. When you meet your date probably she will also be nervous. So **make her feel comfortable** by saying things like you have been looking forward to this all day. The enjoyment will stem from the conversation that you will have on that first date. So prepare on some **safe topics** of conversation like how was her day. Ask her about herself but do not be too intrusive.   Talk about general topics like TV shows, movies books etc till she feels more at ease. Once you **find out** more about **her interests** you will automatically find the conversation flowing. If there is a lull in the conversation, bring up back-up topics like her favorite vacation or places she would like to see. This way your date will start to feel more relaxed and you will find that the first date is going smoothly.

6.3 How to impress your date?

It is important to make your date **feel special** if you want to take the relationship ahead. Remember **who you are** and do not try to be someone else, because your fraudulence will shine through. **Hold her attention** by using your wit, use funny stories, but nothing too dirty, especially on a first date. Dress and look **sophisticated**. No matter what you do for a living, let her know that **you enjoy what you do** and take pride in it. **Do not complain** about everything. Let her know that you are a **fun person** - not someone boring who she has to talk to. Buy her flowers or small **romantic** gifts. Women love to receive them. It shows to her that you were thinking about her while you were apart. Be **courteous**, hold the door and help her with her coat; pull out chairs, do not interrupt her, do not talk on the cellphone on a date, and do not look at other people in the room. Ask her about herself. **Focus on her good qualities**. Don't ask any personal questions. **Make her feel good about herself**. Fish for some common ground for interesting conversation. **Talking** too much **about past**

relationships is a sure way to get rejected by most females!

6.4 How to be Charismatic?

Charisma is a sort of magnetism that inspires confidence and adoration in women. It does not depend on looks, but more on **personality**. Like beauty, luck, and social position, charisma can open many doors in life. However unlike these other qualities, anyone can become more charismatic. Try to be relaxed at all times and look **confident**. If you are anxious, you will channel your anxiety to other people. Charismatic people are **relaxed and calm** under all situations. Being calm and relaxed they are able to channel this energy into other people. This makes them more attractive. Also in your communication with others, treat them as equals and **with respect**. Make each person you meet feel as though he or she is **truly important**, regardless of your first impression or that person's reputation. If you make people feel good about themselves, they'll be drawn to you and hold a higher opinion of you. Be authentic in expressing your views. Try to connect with the emotions of others. Assess their **emotional needs** and respond to their sensitivity with empathy. Be in control of your emotions and express them appropriately. **Speak clearly** with conviction and passion but at a relaxed pace. Developing charisma is an art. Charisma must come **from within you** and must reflect your personality as an individual. Fortunately, everyone has the ability to be charismatic, and it simply needs to be coaxed out. Practice and take note of what works and what needs improvement. **Don't mimic others**. Allow your individuality to set you apart. **Have a message**. If you believe in something or feel strongly about it, communicate that in a respectful way. Your charisma will help people be accepting of your ideas. Take an acting class or public speaking course. Actors and charismatic people use the same techniques to captivate their audience and **evoke emotion**. Some thoughts may be weird, but wording them right can be a bit charming. That is a skill which can be developed through practice. Being charismatic isn't the same as pleasing people. Charismatic people are **courageous** in their outlook and yet respectful of others. **Dropping seriousness and self-concern** makes one more charismatic. Consider your audience and be careful not to offend them. It can be okay to be controversial, but it is not the same as being being offensive. You can easily learn the art of charisma through **self training**.

6.5 How to be Charming?

Charm adds to your personality and will make you more attractive to females. Everyone is born with a certain amount of **natural charm** but it can be enhanced by practice. Effort and careful attention to the **needs and desires of others** will ensure that charm becomes a permanent part of your character. Practice walking with good relaxed **posture** to project self **confidence** (even if you don't feel that way on the inside). Relax the muscles in your face to the point where you have a natural, pleasant expression permanently engraved there. Make **connection** with others by making good eye contact. Nod and smile subtly with a subdued joy shining forth. Be interested in people in general. Talk to others about things which appeal to them. **Praise** others instead of gossiping behind their backs. Everyone will know that their reputation is safe with you. This will increase your **trustworthiness**. Don't Lie. A lie is something you say for which there is some direct evidence somewhere out there that contradicts it. Issue compliments generously, especially to **raise others' self esteem**. Try to pick out something that you appreciate in any situation and verbally express that appreciation. If you like something or someone, find a creative way to say it and say it immediately. Control your **tone of voice** and make it **gentle and peaceful**. Don't complain about life, look at the **positive side** of everything. **Empathy** is at the core of charm. Be patient with others. Avoid arguing with others.

Many people mistake arrogance for charm. In fact, **arrogance is anti-charm**. Charmers live to please others. Arrogant people live to please themselves. Arrogance only attracts insecure people while charm attracts everyone. Wait for your turn in the conversation. **Selflessness** is the best road to charisma. Never listen to any gossip about you and never spread gossip either. This will harm your reputation. **Do not swear or spread rumors**. This is not charming at all. **Avoid talking too much about yourself**. Listen to people instead of talking much. Rather than changing your character to match with someone else's, highlight the good aspects of your own self.

6.6 How to be energetic and fun loving?

Women are drawn to energetic and fun loving men because they are full of positive energy. These people see life as a game to play and enjoy, they radiate good health. They do not entertain negative thinking, are able to

accept themselves for who they are, don't take themselves too seriously and they **see challenges as opportunities** to be creative. We all need to integrate these values in our attitude. We must learn to not take other people's judgments personally. We must learn to **accept the past, live in the present and be positive about the future.** Don't be too sensitive or too worried about the way things are; get the most out of these experiences, even if they aren't entirely pleasant. Think creatively when challenges present themselves. **Forgive yourself and others** when screw ups happen. This lightens your heart and adds tremendous energy to your life. Remember that everyone makes mistakes, including yourself, and learn not to let this anger or upset you beyond the point of forgiveness. Be thankful for all the blessings you have and take care of your body, mind, and spirit. Just enjoy the life energy within yourself. Live every day like it's your last! **Live** as much as possible **in the present, forgetting and forgiving your past** and **not fantasizing too much about the future**. When your thoughts are upbeat, hopeful, contented, inspiring, grateful, and joyous, you exude energy. Then you are naturally and effortlessly a fun loving, energetic person that any women will love to be close with.

6.7 How to be fun and flirty?

Flirting in important to create attraction in females. However too much of anything is bad. Learn to smile, look exciting and happy. During flirting **avoid cheesy pickup lines**. Be original, or you'll look like a fool. **Be yourself** - this is the most important bit. Nobody likes a person who is just a clone; especially when they only do it to impress someone. Laugh a lot, tell jokes, and smile. **Be bright, funny and entertaining.** You should be able to put on a show with your personality. When you are flirting, **smile, wink, and be sweet**! Smile all the time as if the world was smiling with you.

6.8 How to be fun to be with?

Women like to be around men that have a **pleasant lively personality** although they may not be funny in the literal sense. You can incorporate these elements into your personality by following these tips. Firstly **good conversation skills** are crucial when you want to be a likable person, and this includes the ability to listen and respond appropriately. So practice listening carefully to what the the other person is saying. Make good eye contact and give them full attention when they say something. **Smile and laugh** often as it will make women also feel happy. It makes you seem like you truly love life and you can deal with any problems that you have to face. Be a happy **optimistic** person, not a complainer. Also you need to be active and creative. Maybe do a "happy dance" when something good happens, or twirl around to **cheer someone up**. Just be yourself and be a people person. Be friendly, kind, giving, caring, generous, learn about them, and make them want to know more about you. Be mysterious and intriguing at times.

At other times be **spontaneous** and **lighthearted**. No one likes boredom, or to feel like nothing new ever happens. Don't try to forcefully make people think you are fun. It comes off as phony and pushy. **Don't laugh at people. Laugh with them**. It's good to laugh at yourself when you goof up or make mistakes. Be aware that the kind of fun you're having is healthy, legal, and doesn't cause anyone any harm, including yourself. If you are really close, obvious flirtatious teasing is all right. But if you are just getting to know someone, start off polite.

6.9 How to be humorous?

Being funny is generally seen as a desirable quality in the dating world, and it can also help you make friends with females or fit in any social situations. To be naturally funny **think beyond jokes**. Broaden your base of comedy material. In everyday conversation, being funny is mostly about having something funny to say about something that comes up in the course of the conversation. **Watch**

other comedians on TV. Be observant and see the humor in everyday situations. Anything which is **unknown**, the **surprising**, and the **incongruous** are often funny. You can find these by looking, for example, for connections between **dissimilar things** or by looking for the **unexpected in the familiar**. On a more basic level, just pay attention to what **people around you** are saying and doing. **Know your audience**. Different people find different things funny. However **timing** in humor is important. Develop a comic personality by developing your **own unique style of humor**. In other words, learn from comedians and friends, but don't try to copy them (unless you're doing impressions, which can be funny). Forgive yourself when a joke falls flat. Don't be discouraged. Learn from your comedic errors, and keep trying. Don't be afraid to make fun of yourself. **Self-deprecating humor** is a lot safer than making fun of others, and it can be really funny. Just be careful not to sound pathetic or whiny, especially if you're trying to impress a date. When you make jokes about others however, be sure to not insult them and if you are feeling angry, don't let it out through a demeaning joke. **Don't make jokes** or comments about people's **race, religion,** etc.

6.10 How to be happy being yourself?

Being happy in yourself is really cool and attractive to women. This means doing happily what you want, **achieving your goals**, not worry about living up to others expectations because this is your life. You can be happy with yourself only by **accepting yourself** with all your shortcomings. Eliminate people who cannot accept you as you are. **Forget others' opinions**. If you feel fat because someone said you were, they were probably covering up for their own insecurity problem. **Forgive and forget** and **move on**. Everyone makes mistakes. Enjoy yourself because life is short. Live it well. Never back down from an obstacle you face. Always remember, **you are number one priority of your self.** Mistakes happen, people may or may not learn from them. Forgive them. **Try helping others.** There is nothing like helping someone else, because this will improve your own self confidence. Do something that you want to do, or like to do every day. Enjoy the moment of being free, and carry that with you for the rest of the day. It's your life; so live it how you want to! But **be aware and take responsibility** of what you are doing. Your happiness and content with life will be transmitted to all people around you.

6.11 How to be irresistible to women?

Do you have your eye on someone that you would 'really' love to attract in all the right ways? Remember that real relationships are complex things with stuff happening on different levels all at the same time. You can make a woman **dependent on you** if you are following these tips. Be **honest** and show her you **respect her**. Don't play games. Do what you can to catch and keep her attention, but don't play with her mind or her heart. Once you lose a woman's **trust**, it's near impossible to regain it. Don't expect to get laid all the time. Instead **play hard to get** once you have created interest in her. Women can't stand to think that you possibly don't want them. You remain a constant in her mind. But always **be there for her** when she needs you. When she looks upset or sad, gently ask her if she is okay and try to **help her cheer up** by being supportive. At other times **be mysterious** and leave her alone.....it'll make her want you even more. Fill her life with little acts of **surprise and kindness**. This will slowly make her dependent on you.

6.12 How to be Romantic?

The concept of romance can vary from woman to woman. But the central theme involves doing something to express **affection** in a meaningful yet **unexpected** way. A true act of romance requires creativity and sincerity, often inspired by love. Doing something different, something that your partner would not expect. The more out of the ordinary, the better! Treat her with a lot of 'wonder' as though you're trying to earn her affection and trust. **Put on a show**! Make it personal. Think about what really gets that special someone excited. Recognize what makes your **partner unique**, and do things for them that only they would appreciate. Being romantic means **acknowledging how special** a person is, and that means **demonstrating** that **you know, better than anyone else** in the world, what makes them unique. Focus on the little things. Romance can be practiced every day, and it doesn't have to be expensive or grand. In fact, sometimes the most romantic moments are simple, spontaneous and free. Be sincere to make her feel appreciated, truly **be thankful for her presence in your life**. Surprise your partner by doing something you would never normally do on your own, just because you know it'd make them happy. If your partner doesn't seem to appreciate your efforts, it's not that you've failed to be romantic; it's that your partner has failed to receive your affection. Maybe they're not accustomed to being romanced, or maybe they're distracted by other stresses in their lives. If you feel rejected, don't just give up. Talk to her about it. **Being romantic doesn't mean being obsessive**. There is a difference between expressing appreciation and expecting a person to devote all of their time to you in return. Remember you are an individual, not just one half of a relationship.

6.13 How to make her laugh?

One of the quickest and easiest ways to a girl's heart is to make her laugh and smile. It's easy to entertain her with **witty conversation** in your interactions. Be confident, but not overly confident, because that could appear arrogant. Here are some suggestions to increase your sense of humor. Combine funny dialogue, subtle jokes and witty one-liners to showcase your sense of humor and completely charm the woman you hope to win. In order to be make her laugh you need to be able to think on your feet. It is not that difficult. Just observe the environment and look for clues. Read witty pieces and watch comedians on TV. See how they **exaggerate and fantasize** on common day to day activities to create humor. Develop a vocabulary of funny phrases and gags. Practice maintaining a straight face when you deliver **punch lines**. Tell **embarrassing stories** about your childhood, humorous mistakes you've made or a mishap that occurred this morning. A self-deprecating sense of humor can be charming as long as it's not overdone. You don't want to undercut her good impression of you. Pay close attention to the conversation to find appropriate spots for comical one-liners. Familiarize yourself with **her favorite** topics, television shows, hobbies, movies and books so you'll be able to use references that will make her laugh. Make playful **observations** as you watch people. Discuss what you assume they're thinking, planning to do or do for a living. Keep the comments harmless, however, so the woman doesn't think you're simply being mean. However be careful of what you say. Perfect your **timing and delivery**. Discover when to make witty comments and when to be serious. If you're "on" all the time, it will seem like you're **trying too hard** (which is a definite turn off). It's time to stop clowning around when her laughter sounds forced. Don't rely on playful insults, sarcastic comments or off-color jokes until you get to know the woman better. What one might find funny another might consider insulting or hurtful. You don't want to hurt her feelings or make a comment that will make you look like a drum-beater. Know when to stop, a good joke can turn bad just by one extra thing you just "had" to say. Be aware that having a good sense of humor could be dangerously attractive to women.

6.14 How to date on a budget?

Dating can be done on a budget if you plan it according to your means. First find out what your partner is **interested in**. The first date should be a meeting to see if you both enjoy the same things and how well you relate to each other. Scan the **newspapers** for interesting places to visit. There usually is a concert in the park, or perhaps in the Mall. This can be great fun and is an inexpensive 'date'. This also could be quite romantic, if you hold hands while walking to find a seat, or just walking the Mall. For women who like the **outdoors**, spend the day on a nature trail, in the park, or on the beach and pack a picnic lunch with their favorite foods to make it extra special. Show your partner **affection** and let them know you love having them close. Remember that if you are planing on a long term relation, each partner should enjoy the other's company, not the lifestyle this person can provide. If you are supposed to pay all the time, just for the honor of having the other persons company, that relation is probably worthless and dangerous.

Section 7 : Getting Physical

7.1 How to break the touch barrier?

In order to get physical with any woman, one has to break the touch barrier carefully **without** making **her** feel **uncomfortable**. First **test the waters with perfect manners** when you're just getting to know each other. Example, offer your hand when she might need to keep her balance, hold out your elbow as an invitation for her to hook her arm around yours, hold out your hand so you can walk through the crowd without losing each other. Look for anything that may be on her face or hair, then ask her to stay still, and gently pull it out. Notice something on her hands like a different ring, a new cut, or a different nail color, ask if you can look closer. Inspect whatever is different, briefly rub her hand gently and let it go. If it's chilly outside and you notice that she's cold or shivering, first offer her your coat, then put it around her. Another great place for casual physical contact is **partner**

dancing or contact sports. If she responded positively to all of the above, make your next move (or risk forever being trapped in the "friend" zone). Try putting your arm around her shoulder or waist, or holding her hand. Most of all, relax, and **pay attention to her demeanor**. Just slowly build up closer intimacy **without seeming desperate** or making her uncomfortable.

7.2 How to make the first move?

If you like her and is afraid to make the first move, this piece will give you an idea of dealing with this issue. Before initiating any kind of move, **look for body language clues** such as prolonged eye contact to help you work out whether you'll get a positive response. **Approach with caution.** Try lightly touching **less intimate areas** of the body- such as the upper arm, or the outer leg nearest to you. If they haven't rejected your advances so far, then you can start to feel more confident about stealing a kiss. If she is co-operative just **continue**

slowly taking it further.

7.3 How to have a first Kiss?

Kissing a woman you have recently met can be a daunting challenge. This article can help you. Remember that most women want you to kiss them. So don't be shy. Before you make a move, make sure your **breath** is clean and you **lips moist** (may be carry lip balm). Also respect her **privacy**. Watch for signals, note her body language for **clues**. Watch her closely and look for the telltale signs that she wants to kiss you like - looking at you lips, licking her lips and or biting her bottom lip. **Ask yourself** these questions - did you and your date seem to have a cozy, warm, close time together? Has she been flirting with you through body language? Has she licked her lips, or bit her lower lip while looking at you? Has she found excuses to touch you often? If you feel confident of these things, prepare to kiss! Make **eye contact**. If she is **comfortable** and doesn't look away then she is ready.

Approach the kiss **with confidence**. Once you've chosen the right moment to kiss someone, there's no turning back, especially if it's your first time kissing that particular person. Be decisive and confident. To begin with touch the woman lightly on the arm or shoulder when you're talking. Just make it a quick, **innocent touch** and don't make a big deal out of it. **Holding hands** is also a good way to break the touch barrier. If everything is going well, try kissing the person on the **cheek**. Go in for a gentle kiss on the cheek and see how they respond. Look at their lips. Make eye contact and then move your gaze briefly down to the woman's lips. Then move your eyes back up to meet theirs and smile seductively. You don't have to be really obvious about it. If the person **doesn't want the kiss**, she will let you know, but until then, act as though you're a pro. Lean in slowly. Make it slow, nice, easy, romantic. Hold her gently. Reach around her waist, gently draw her towards you. Look into her eyes again to let her know that you are really seeing her. Look at her lips. Lean in, and go in for the kiss. An excellent first kiss is one that is **romantic, tender** and memorable. Your **mouth** should not be overly opened or closed, and it shouldn't be mushy or too tight (relax). Don't let it go too long or let it be too short - think around ten seconds or so. A tiny hint of **tongue** is nice if she seems willing, but make it flirtatious and not insistent. Wait for her response. Just remain silent and smile, better yet hug her, **ending** the first kiss in a lovely, intimate moment. Just **be mindful of her reaction**. If she pulls away, or is surprised or otherwise not interested in the kiss, be mature about it and don't take it personally. You can try again later!

7.4 How to Romantically hug a woman?

A romantic hug is a great **prelude to a make-out** session. Make sure you are in a **private comfortable** place alone with the woman. **Ask** for a hug and stand up. Act like you are giving a **regular hug**. Place one arm under hers, in the lower half of her ribcage. Put your other hand on the general area of the shoulder blade. When you hug her, be **slow, gentle, and firm**. Pull her towards you and squeeze. Slowly rub your hands up and down her back and rub your bodies together. Don't be afraid to explore with your hands, but if you are getting a vibe that she might not like it, slow down. If you know her really well, gently put a leg around her and pull her close. Slowly guide her to a comfortable surface. Sit her down on your lap while slowly turning her head towards yours. Kiss her passionately while still rubbing her back with your arms, give her a little massage. **Intensify the kiss** as you slowly put her underneath you. After that you should put your hand on her butt and squeeze, then get your tongue in her mouth deep. Use your arms and legs to rub her and your bodies together. Don't be afraid to **express your pleasure.** Smile at her between kisses. **Don't force anything.** Don't say anything that will spoil the mood. Ensure that your 'comfortable surface' is big enough, you would hate to accidentally push your girlfriend off a sofa or couch. If you go all the way, **use protection**.

Section 8: Rejection & Confidence

8.1 How to handle rejection?

Rejection is painful as it hurts our sense of self. But in dating which is a number game, it is a reality which **cannot be ignored**. In fact rejection in other aspects of life are also painful. But, upsetting as it is, the more we deal with it, the more we become **resilient** to it. In fact we become more adventurous if we learn to deal with rejection appropriately. These tips will help you to better handle rejection in the dating scene. **Everyone** has faced rejection at some point of their life. So we must acknowledge that anyone can be rejected, no matter who they are. Eventually we must **learn to move on**. Think of knocking on another door - if you keep trying, soon you will find a new door opening after the old door is closed in your face. Maybe you did miss out on something you wanted, but you're past that and the new door could be much better. **Accept your feelings**. Cry, let your feelings out and talk to your supportive friends about your rejection. **Keep trying**. Getting rejected is a natural component of picking up women. It's trial and error, and everyone fails in this process from time to time. **Don't keep ruminating over your failures.** Just keep in mind – it is all a number game and practice different approaches to **find out what works for you best.** The past does not necessarily equal the future. If you look at rejection as a trivial side issue and persist with your game, **you will be rewarded**. Rejection is a **lesson** in becoming a **strong and confident** person. In time you will learn how to ignore rejection and keep trying again. No matter what, **don't give up**. Always remember after every rejection that picking-up females is just a number game!

8.2 How to overcome the fear of rejection?

Fear of rejection can **prevent you from meeting** new women. When you look deeply within yourself, you will realize that this fear is based on the idea that some woman has the **power over you to control** or decide how you feel about yourself. Overcoming this fear involves accepting yourself and **regaining control** over your emotions. Believe that you can take care of yourself. Being too dependent on what others think can cause more fear of rejection. **You cannot control what goes on inside the mind of other people. However it is up to you to control what goes on inside your mind.** If you **do not** consider yourself to **be too desperate** for any particular woman and instead focus on developing your dating skills, you will find it more helpful. The more desperate you feel, the more you may be afraid of rejection. Instead **enjoy the process of learning** rather than focusing on the outcome. Define your **self-image** based on your good inner qualities rather than external opinion. **Focus on your inner qualities** like being honest, treating people with kindness and being generous. Overcoming fear of rejection requires that **you're secure with who you are**. When you know that your self-image is unaffected by other people's opinion, you don't fear their rejection any longer. View any rejection as an **opportunity to grow** and improve further. You can always control certain aspects of your appearance, your behavior, your intelligence and your personality. Look at rejection as constructive criticism and incorporate the cause of the rejection into a plan to evolve. **Praise yourself for trying**. The more you handle rejection, the easier it gets to approach any situation where you may be rejected and the closer you come to overcoming this fear of rejection. Set a goal to get few rejections every day. You may get a positive response or you may gain experience in surviving a rejection. You need to **reward yourself for the effort** and focus on the fact that you tried rather than the actual results. Trust this approach, it is scientifically called '**desensitization**'. With time you will be in full control over your fear.

8.3 How to get over rejection?

You may experience the sense of rejection every time

you go into a situation that doesn't go as you expected. Rejection may leads you to believe that you are unwanted, unworthy or not valuable. If you've been rejected, your self-esteem may be hurt. Luckily there are effective psychological techniques to overcome rejection. First you need to realize that rejection is a person's **individual opinion based on individual preferences -** and these can vary with upbringing, socio-cultural background, life experiences etc. Rejection stems from that person's way of looking at life. You must be able to accept that person's opinion as just another point of view and not an absolute fact written in stone. **Value your good qualities** and **focus on your strengths** as an individual to overcome the feeling of rejection. Make a list of things that you like about yourself and review it daily. You need to look at areas where you have great potential and strive to achieve it. Doing something 'noble' for someone, like volunteering for some great cause can help you cultivate your positive qualities. Make a conscious choice to overcome 'any' type of rejection that you may face in life. Everyone is bound to feel hurt or disappointed at several points in time. You have the choice to look at rejection as an opportunity to grow and better yourself or allow it to consume you. You need to accept that you are capable of change when change is needed. However, you must also realize that **sometimes rejection is the result of the other person's (woman's) inability to change** and is a flaw within them, not you. Many people believe in something larger than man's free-will, whether it's a higher power defined by an organized religion or something more personal. Having belief in something larger than you can allow you to gain perspective on rejection. Many people look at rejection as part of destiny and learn to accept it as part of existence. Get professional counseling if you feel very depressed, more than you can handle on your own. The degree of pain caused by rejection directly correlates to how intimate you were with the person who rejected you. Many people need to get **professional help** to overcome rejection from a spouse or a long term partner after relationship breakdown. Explore the different options if you decide to get outside professional help.

8.4 How to tell when you may have been rejected by a woman?

Let us look at a situation when you finally work up the nerves to ask your person of interest (crush) to go out on a date with out. She politely declines. Wait - were you really rejected? Read on to find out if you should give it **another shot.** What does your gut tell you? Sometimes we so much want a relationship to work that we gloss over the reality of the situation. Take a deep breath and try to **evaluate** with a clear mind whether or not this person is that into you or not. In addition to your gut, test your body temperature. Research has shown that feelings of rejection actually cause a person's body temperature to drop. If unsure whether your heartthrob's stare was actually a glare, check to see if you felt a chill. **Put yourself in the other person's shoes.** If you're naturally outgoing, is it possible the other person is the shy type and not actually ignoring you? Or, if you asked someone out on a date and she declined because she had to do something important, ask yourself if that person's explanation is possible. If so, chances are that you were not rejected. Did you notice **any lying cues** this person might have, like face reddening or avoiding eye contact? If the reason she turned you down seemed dubious, it just might be. Rather than spending sleepless nights wondering whether or not you were rejected, you might as well ask. If the answer is yes, perhaps you triggered a red flag in this person's mind, and you two weren't meant to be. If you misunderstood and your crush did not reject you after all, well, you'll be happy you asked! Likewise, check in with your friends. They might offer insight which is up to you to take or reject. **Give it some time.** Often whether or not a relationship works is because of timing. Maybe she had a bad day. Maybe she recently broke up with someone else. If she rejected you the first time, maybe after some time apart and distance, the outcome will be different. If you did suffer a rejection, you're not alone! Most people have been rejected at some point in their lives. Remember, there are plenty of fish in the sea, and the timing just might not be right. Give yourself a pat on the back for going boldly in search of love!

8.5 How to move on after rejection?

Rejection is a type of 'loss'. When you are reading this may be you are thinking of some experience from your life. Again accept this as normal and read the tips given here. Hopefully, reading this part of the book will change your perspective on the lost relationship and make you stronger for the future. **It happens to everyone and you are certainly not alone.** Even though you may feel sad and demoralized, you will eventually move on and be a stronger person. **Time is a great healer.** Heal yourself by learning to **forgive yourself**. Your sense of self has been hurt. **Accept that** you are a human being and it is okay to feel pain. **Nothing to be ashamed of! Remove her memories** from your life by deleting things which remind you of the wound. What goes on inside the mind of others is not really within our direct control. Yes we may have influence over it, but still it is not within our control. **Different people have different preferences.** Some people like oranges and some like apples. Like that if someone likes oranges and hates apples, that does not mean that everyone will think in the same way. Similarly if some person rejects you, it does not mean that everyone else with reject you in future as well. That is simply impossible! Remember the age old saying: "there are plenty of fish in the sea" **Don't waste time thinking** of her, just try to move on. If you do not hang on to her memories, if you **let go** of them, you will realize that your pain is gone. Remember – the 'Number Game'!

8.6 How to regain confidence after rejection?

Treat others with kindness and you will find that how

you do unto others controls what you think others will do unto you. To gain confidence, remind yourself that you like to help other people and listen to them when they come to you. You may know deep down that you are a worthy person but a setback or difficult time in the past may be holding you back. **Be accommodating and compassionate towards your own self.** Gain confidence by doing nice things for other women you know, and by **being truthful with yourself.** The next time someone asks you to do something you aren't comfortable with, politely say no instead of unwillingly saying yes. **Once you have rejected a few people yourself, it will be easier to accept rejection from others** without totally losing your confidence. If you are not a very confident person, it is going to be really scary the first few times you get rejected. In these situations **think of a confident person who inspires you** and act as much like him as you. Eventually it will get easier to be confident and you can do it without adopting a false persona. **Develop a thick skin**, remember the concept of the number game.

Confident sales people don't let rejection or setbacks bother them. Try your best **not to take these things personally** - eventually you will have more successes than failures and it will be easier to deal with rejection.

Section 9: Conclusion

Being able to influence women requires a lot of different **social** skills and **psychological** techniques. One of the best ways to do this is to **practice** your skills **daily on every woman** you come across. With practice you'll develop more comfort in a variety of situations, and when you become comfortable, you'll naturally **be yourself**. Start with the **SOFTEN** (Smile, Open posture, Forward lean, Touch, Eye contact, Nod) approach and see how she responds. Take **one step at a time** but keep practicing day in and day out. Do not show women that you are needy or desperate. **Neediness** can be a vicious cycle. You seek attention, the woman gets spooked and pushes you away, you feel worse about yourself, and you're even needier the next time around. Instead learn to **value yourself**! Learn **self-control**. Imagine your interaction with any woman is like a tennis game. Every time you initiate contact, your throw the ball to her side of the court. Then, you have to wait for her to send it back. You don't toss a whole bunch more just to make sure she is still interested in playing. If you're a little on the needy side, you probably get nervous and worried while you're waiting. When this happens, **take a deep breath**. Look at the options, if they return the ball then the game continues. If not there are many others who are waiting to play the game. Also if someone doesn't have the decency to respectfully respond, they're not worth your time. You deserve better than that. So **respect yourself** and move on without wasting time. It is a **number game** and there are plenty of fish in the sea!

You can do It.!

REQUEST FOR FEEDBACK

Dear Reader,

We value your Feedback.

On behalf of the authors we would like to listen to your comments. We are continuously trying to improve the self-help training products created by us to suit the needs of beginners. Our purpose is to generate **Easy** and **Effective training material** which can cater to the requirements of those who are new to the Pickup Game.

We would request you to give your comments about this book on its web-page by using the *'Customer Review'* section.

Please tell us what you thought of the product as this will help us and possibly other customers as well. We will apply your suggestions to create improved products in future to suit your particular requirements.

Your Satisfaction is our Inspiration.

Thank you, **Publisher.**

7485090R0

Made in the USA
Lexington, KY
28 November 2010